Contents

Preface iv
Dedication vii
The Party Girl: Finding My Spirit 1
The Perfect Girl: Then and Now 5
I Love My Real World Life as a Little Girl During the 1950s 9
My Star Flickers and Shines Bright – Boy or Girl or Both? 13
I am so Truly Black and White 17
My Wonderful Mom 21
Flight 911: Saving The World, Pass it Forward 25
Learning to Conquer Social Love and Fear: Inside and Outside
   at the Dinner Dance 29
Poetic Memoirs of a Geisha 33
Life is a Rainbow 37
New Vision: Now My Life
   Torch Is Ever So Brightly Shimmering 43

Preface

My SHIMMERING STAR was bright. I loved my youth. I adored my family, my parents and my friends as a child and young adult. They were my shimmering stars that shined so bright for me. I became an elementary school teacher and I loved my school kids.

But my personal star faded out in my mid-life crisis, and I sank into a pit of despair. But my star was not extinct. I had to climb out of my Grand Canyon to rediscover myself, redefine myself, and renew my eternal love for people and life.

Now I am on again on track to follow my SHINING SHIMMERING STAR path to the Wizard of Oz, on the yellow brick road.

Now also, New Vision: Now My Life Torch Is Ever So Brightly Shimmering.

I thank my friends, my mentors and my family who encouraged me to not give up but to let my star shine once again. I love you all and know that you are the ones who really "Light up My Life." I will never forget you.

So Bright My Shimmering Star

The New Millenium Is Here For Me
November 6, 2000

Today is my Shimmering Star
July 21, 2006

By
Debere Worley-Heard

I finally arrived at the top of the Grand Canyon!

My star was shimmering so bright on my wedding day, Saturday, December 27, 2008

Aspect Books

**PRINTED IN
THE UNITED STATES OF AMERICA**

World rights reserved. This book or any portion thereof may not be copied or reproduced in any form or manner whatever, except as provided by law, without the written permission of the publisher, except by a reviewer who may quote brief passages in a review.

The author assumes full responsibility for the accuracy of all facts and quotations as cited in this book.

Copyright © 2011 Aspect Books
ISBN-13: 978-1-57258-548-5
Library of Congress Control Number: 2011903543

Published by
Aspect Books

Debere in her 4th, 5th, and 6th grade Developmentally Handicapped classroom at Pickett Elementary School during 1982.

Debere as classroom teacher at Picket Elementary with student teacher from Bowling Green State University.

Dedication

I shall dedicate this book I created to my family and friends:
- My Godmothers – Ella P. Stewart and Vernetta Watson
- My Godfather – Talmadge Watson
- My Grandmother – Elnora Mitchell
- My great Grandfather – Mack Mitchell
- My Parents – Thomas Daniel and Dorothy Mae Worley
- My Brother – Michael McKinley Worley
- My Honorary Mother - Ann Veasey
- Spiritual Mothers – Mattie Fuller, Elaine Barton
- Younger Brother – Tiger
- Oldest Sister – Delores
- Big Sister – Gina Spears Wilson
- Spiritual Sisters – Jeanette Edmonds, Ella Pickett
- My Cousins – Jessie Beck and family, AD and family, Michael and Sheila Doles and Sandra Smith
- My Sister-In-law – Deinese Scott Worley
- My Husband – Raymond Heard and his family: Gregory, Reginald, Kevin, Rupert, Gerard, Bernard, Shannette, and Spouses & Grandchildren
- My Mentors – Big Bear (Barry), Dr. Curtis Lewis, Wayne Graham, Joseph Spaulding, Father Buff, Father Nelson, Father Kimble, Father Dave Beck
- My High School and College Friends – Robbie Todd, Engrid Haynes, Gail Sanders, Rose Bud (from India), Tito (from the Phillipines), Satita (from China), Lee (from Taiwan), Katie

and Joseph (from Barbados)
- My Parents' Friends – Nola and Homer Wilford, Naomi and Howard Goings, Rosco and Marian Doles, Katherine and Robert Glover, Mr. and Mrs. George Lindsey, Mr. and Mrs. Aubrey Buffkin
- My Current Friends – Daniel Dawson and family, Lois Austin, Peggy Sue Atkins and family
- My neighbors in the 900 Block of Carver Blvd – Mrs. Willa Thomas and family, Judy Milstein and Terisa Scircle, Miss Anthony, Dr. John Wiley, Linda Florian, Barbara and Jarvis Wynn, Officer Madison, Hershal Davis.
- My Childhood Friends – Robby Todd Casper, Kathy Hankins, Janice Pleasant McWilliams
- My best animal Friends – Coco Gigit Lynn, T.J. Tyson Worley, Sugar Love Mae Bejóncé, Star Iesia, Princess Kitty
- My Medical Doctors – Drs. Kirshner, Hammersly, Santora, Olson, Pinsky, Abbo, Daniels, Ahrens, Mohamed, Jamie Ruiz, Balae, Rubie Knuckoes, D.A. Hernandez, Alson, Yoon, Willey, Anna Mae Newton, Michael Fitzpatrick, John Wiley and my pulmonary technicians Pat and John and Dr. Edna Jean
- My Therapist – Jean Babalos
- My Memorable Student – Kevin Campbell and his mother Martha Campbell and family
- My Elementary School Teachers – Mrs. Hopkins (5th grade), Mrs. Louise Parks (7th grade), Mrs. Ardella Reed (8th grade), Mrs. Craynon (2nd grade), Miss Winigar (1st grade)
- My God Child - Halée Kristina Arnett
- My God Child - Sam

As you can see, my star shimmers ever so bright while heading out to Putin bay.

I also wish to thank these public schools, the educators, the colleges, the universities and the societies, who annointed me with significant knowledge, wisdom and experience to enhance my life and my happiness and my joy:

- Wayne Graham
- University of Toledo (now merged with Medical University of Ohio) – including sorority/fraternity societies: AKA (Alpha Kappa Alpha), Delta, Alpha Phi Alpha, Omega PSI Phy
- Bowling Green
- Toledo public schools
- The Crosby Gardens
- The Toledo Zoological Society
- The Toledo Art Museum

THANK YOU ALL FOR ADDING
MEANING AND JOY TO MY LIFE

Chapter 1

The Party Girl: Finding My Spirit

In The Beginnng: The Party Kid

Whoopie! I am 6 years old and I am invited to a big adult party. My father's employer was having a party, for his son's Fraternity organization, on his big yacht, called "The First Blast." My brother, aged 12, escorted me there, and it is my first big party I remember as a child. I felt really comfortable being with my brother at this party. I am so happy; I love to be with such people and I feel so proud. I am really ready to party!

It was great fun. I had the opportunity to meet really nice people and to eat some superb food. The yacht was tied to a dock on the Maumee River, in back of a neighbor's back yard. I was around the very rich of the rich, on a 60-foot yacht. The sun was shining so brightly. My father adored me and was very supportive of me in attending this event. Both of my parents were proud of me, wanted the best for me, and wanted to show me off to their friends. This great party started me thinking: "Am I up to the task of becoming a 'Party Girl'?"

I quickly concluded, "Yes I am! That's me! I love to party. I am a

So Bright My Shimmering Star

Party Girl."

I always loved to attend parties as a kid. Birthday parties, Sunday School parties, school parties. You name it, I was there—always feeling happy, on a high, and loving people. Any yes, trying my best. Even 12 years later at my own . . .

High School Graduation Party

It was a real blast. My parents held it for me at our home, and all the neighbors and family friends were there—they were the ones who watched me grow up on a daily basis. And my personal friends were there too. Everyone was so happy; We danced, sang, nibbled and had fun all night, til the early morn. I received so many gifts and tons of cards with money! I was really being treated so great, and that forever made me feel like a special, blessed, party girl. I was really on a high and positive spirit at that moment. My motto was:

I love people. I love to be with them, interact, tell jokes, dance and be happy. I like the positive mood, the joy of happiness, the presence of others. That is all I really need . . . to " party" with people. I must be becoming A PARTY WOMAN.

My College Days: Learning the Collegiate Way

Six months later, I was attending BGSU (Bowling Green University) for my undergraduate career, also as a "College Party Girl." Many parties were sponsered on campus by fraternities. They were really fun. My first one was given by the Alpha Phi Alpha fraternity. Lots of dancing, drinking and eating. There was my first nemesis—the punched bowl, spiked of course. They warned me not to have more than one, but I was a novice and did not listen to their advice. I had three - maybe more. Then I found out what it was like to be high—for the very first time in my life! But just my luck, my body did not cooperate. Everything I had eaten that night was eliminated in a matter of seconds. I now had my experience with the reality of feeling drunk.

I learned my lesson that night. Never more than two drinks. That worked for me. The rest of my parties were smooth, but . . .

I did not know the heartbreak and suffering which I would begin to encounter in the near future, during my college career. I would be successful, become a career teacher, but my ability to party one-on-one with the opposite sex, would lead me to suffering . . . but that is another story.

My Party Girl Re-emerges: Recapturing My Spirit

It is 20+ years later than my undergraduate college days, with a lot of water under the bridge, having passed me by. I have suffered some bad experiences and disability. I have had some bad judgement and bad luck in judging male suitors, and I wound up with an empty bag and some years of depression and regret.

But now I am on track to recapture my Shining Twinkling Star once again. My inner Spirit propels me to action.

I wish to become a real Party Girl again. What should I do?

PARTY GIRL REDEFINED: I know who I am. I know what I need now. I know what I really love to do.

- PEOPLE WHO LIKE PEOPLE - to be with them, to help them with their problems and needs, to teach them what I have learned in life. I feel I am strong enough to do that again now.
- TO DREAM ABOUT IDEAL LOVE - to continue my fantasies about perfect love and life because it makes me feel good, even with my feet on the ground.
- TO PARTY EVERY DAY - my party is my mood, my feelings, my happiness. It is my desire to celebrate my life and my loves which remain. It is my destiny to be a positive and

So Bright My Shimmering Star

    uplifting person as I started out to be in my life.

I cannot continue to question my destiny . . .

I wish to count my blessings that I have rediscovered . . . I want to party to celebrate my zest and love of life.

Thank you, Father, for helping me feel happy again.

Chapter 2

The Perfect Girl: Then and Now

By Debere L. Worley
October 20, 2000

Then

It was a bright sunshiny Sunday, and I was dressed in my pink outfit with my pink hat and bow, on my way to church. My Mom and Dad looked at me and said "Debbie, make sure you behave perfectly, because your wonderful Godmother Dr. . . . is going to be there also." I looked at myself in the mirror, and examined every inch of my hair, face and dress to make sure that I was perfect. I was 8 years old, and my parents loved me very much. I knew I had to be good, always say and do the right things, and be the model of perfect looks and behavior that they expected, and which I also expected from myself.

I arrived at the church, with my bouquet of flowers in my hand. I held the flowers, right in front of me, with both my hands clamped on the bouquet - because I knew it had to be perfectly symmetrical as I once saw in an easter picture. I stood by the church with my parents and godmother, watching the other children my age go by; as I saw

So Bright My Shimmering Star

them float on by, I noticed their clothes were wrinkled, their hair was mussed up and some of them did not hold their bodies perfectly erect as I was, or restrain their loud behavior. I said to myself, "hmmf, what is wrong with those creatures, why can't they be more perfect; I have to be and will be perfect, to make up for them and to keep my parents and Godmother loving me!"

Fast forward to my college campus 15 years later. I am walking along with my books in my arms. The grass is green, the Spring flowers are blooming everywhere and I have my smile on my face. Two male students are sitting on the bench watching me walk. They stop me on the way and say, "Hey, baby, you look good. Do you want to come to our party tonight?"

I knew these guys, having seen them hang around before, watching girls and joking to each other. I thought to myself, "Hmmf, these guys are playboys. They are not good enough or serious enough for me. I do not need them, or have the time to go to a fraternity party." So I said to them as I passed them by "Hey, you boys should be in class, instead of looking for girls to party with—shame on you!"

And so I went on in my life. Keeping my standards up to the sky as my limit. I acted and felt that I would need to find the best, the brightest and the nicest man around. My search continued a long time . . . and I rejected many observers and a few suitors along the way. Some of them deserved to be rejected, I do know for sure. Most of them never really were given the opportunity by me to even be scrutinized by my standards, as my rapid gaze or attitude passed them by.

And so I wound up years later with an empty bag and a confidence level that took a gradual downward spiral, as my loneliness began to grow and my backward reflections took on a new view of myself . . .

The Perfect Girl: Then and Now

Now

I am standing in front of my Monday night three-hour Therapy Group (for which I am a member), giving a five-minute lecture.

They have noticed over the last six months how much my spirits and behavior have risen, how much happier I appear and talk, and how my manner and confidence is once again uplifting and positive. My goal at the moment is to explain to them and share what I have learned over the last five years. Especially over the last six months, as I began and continued my dramatic escape from my desperate odyssey—the pit at the bottom of the Grand Canyon Pit of Despair. But now I am climbing out of the Pit as I have decided I would rather be facing once again toward the Sun of Happiness, to Light up my Life and feel my eternal love of life . . .

My lecture begins with "Being happy with yourself is a matter of defining who you are. Once you can do that, or redo that, then you can understand what is important to yourself - what are your values, what makes you happy, and what you want to do. Once you stop feeling sorry for yourself, give up the magical thinking and regrets of the past, then you are free to start again. And yes, God has given us the option to start again, to regain what we love, to do what gives us excitement, joy and satisfaction. God knows that we must forgive ourselves first, and recapture the essence of our soul, for he knows that He has give each of us human beings the ability to love and to be loved by each other as well as by ourself. I myself have been fortunate enough to once again realize that people do love me for who I am, despite my long depression, despite my failure to continue in my career as a grade school teacher and despite my self-perceived failure to ever marry and have my own family. I thank the Lord now for giving me the strength to climb up once again toward the golden Sun of Life . . ."

Now I am waiting near my phone for my Mentor to call me again from across the country. He became a supporter to me this year, and has helped me see myself, to redefine myself and to inspire me to get back on my feet. My Mentor has become a pen-pal, a Friend and a Brother to me by being open, honest, and caring about my future. My Mentor has come to know who I am, my values and my character as well as my history and need for perfection in my life. But most importantly, my mentor has strongly told me how much admiration and positive attitude he has about me as a person and how much it would mean to him and the world to see me climb out of my Grand Canyon. He inspired me to try, he cheered me along the way, he pushed and pulled me up the cliff. And he told me how much love I had inside me which I needed to share with others. Then I reached enough momentum to propel me faster. Now I continue to climb on my own . . .

Moving to the Future

I am determined to be happy in my life. I am still stuck in my infant paradigm of striving to be the PERFECT GIRL, but now I have my feet firmly on the ground—my mentor helped me to put them there again. Now I know that I must balance being perfect with being realistic, brave and less critical of myself for making mistakes, and having lost a decade of my life.

I want to believe, I need to believe, I will believe in my quest for life and love.

I am grateful to God for saving me from myself and from never having learned to be a more balanced person, even if it meant not being perfect. Now I understand. Now I wish to continue my life and feel joy.

And now I still want to say again, "I love you, Mom and Dad. You were wonderful to me, and now I want to be wonderful to myself."

Chapter 3

I Love My Real World Life as a Little Girl During the 1950s

Who Am I? The year is now 2004.

I was asked in my parenting class if I was adopted? I answered, "I don't really know. However, if I wasn't I would automatically say no. So I guess there is a possibility that I was adopted. So I might be? Now I know I have some issues to solve?"

This year, I finally really know that there is nothing really wrong with me. My brothers have helped me become strong again, and believe in myself and behave myself, as I did as a little girl in the 1950s.

I was just born with a silver spoon in my mouth. I am really very wealthy, and do not always realize that, or count that blessing.

I had one father who gave me his name and raised me. I had another father who was a biological donor. He made sure I had everything, and the rest of my family had everything too. They all loved me very much. We lived a wonderful American life.

So Bright My Shimmering Star

My Memories

WE WERE FORTUNATE: We had a wonderful pink and white Ford and a second hand green Chevy. We ate lamb chops once a week. We went to church once per week. We went to a wonderful school system that was predominantly white. The yellow and black school bus used to pick us up. We really had a good life going for us at the time.

WE WERE NORMAL HUMANS: Mom and Dad had their ups and downs. One day Dad was so mad at Mom that, to keep from hitting Mom, he picked up the whole full size bed and dropped it on the floor. It made such a loud noise, it scared me to death. I was right there next to Dad when that happened. Mom later left for work. My brother and I stayed with my father the remainder of the day. We played outside the big house. We had a grand old time. We belonged to my dad for the remainder of the day and, as a matter of fact, for the rest of his life and forever.

WE LOVED OUR DAD. HE LOVED US SO MUCH. But we were not aware that we had two fathers . . .

MY BROTHER AND I LOVED TURTLES: We created great games, to play all over the estate that we grew up on. We had fun climbing trees, playing hide and seek. We caught turtles all day! Well, my brother really caught all of the turtles, but he shared them with me. We kept them as pets and fed them ground beef once per day. After the novelty of the turtles expired within us, we later let them go back into the lake, to give them back their freedom—just as Dr. Martin Luther King had preached.

MY BROTHER AND I LOVED IGLOOS AND ANGELS: We used to build snow igloos in the winter, and make snow balls, then have snowfights. Last we then made Snow Angels—which is why I loved angel statues and collected them for the rest of my life. Our childhood was so much fun . . .

I Love My Real World Life as a Little Girl During the 1950s

I wish I could have stayed as a child forever.

It was so much fun being a kid, and I remember my happiness and joy as a kid. But I learned and experienced that it was not as much fun to become a grown-up adult. Adults had always the stress of working, trying to make the best living for all of us. My parents were always trying to please us, by working from sun-up to sun-down.

BUT ONLY NOW, DO I KNOW HOW DIFFERENT I AM: People have always looked at me in astonishment. I saw that look on their faces. People always were happy to see me and talk to me. I remember that always. But only now, have I discovered the truth and only now do I realize:

I Was Famous My Entire Life

The aura I gave off was so innocent and pure. I made everyone feel good when I came around to see them. People loved being around me all the time.

Maybe one day I can become a comedian. Or better yet . . . I can become an ambassador.

I will be what I must be.

With my brother and I knowing everything, made our life so good for us. We enjoyed all the good things in life, while my parents were probably going through a real performance of William Shakespeare. What would you do if you were my mom and dad at that time during the '50s? Remember our country was going through the civil rights movements at that particular historical era. During the '50s, it was hard being colored, which was the word used back then, for Black people. There were separate restaurants, fountains, etc. Separate churches too. Just put yourself in my Mom and Dad's place. Take out a sheet of paper and draw what you would do if you were in my Mom and Dad's place:

So Bright My Shimmering Star

    I am sure my parents were very frightened. But never showed us how much they were. They continued to struggle for happiness. They put us first and kept us on a pedestal. I believe we were on a train to freedom. We could smell freedom everywhere we went. We were not being raised like the typical colored children during the 50s era. It will be phenomenal for the thought of how we will be when we grow up. I believe many people were fantasizing to be able to do the same thing as us.

    I always wanted to be great. My brother always knew he would be great. Now I know we really have been great and have been blessed with an unusual and good life.

THANK YOU, MOM;
THANK YOU, DAD;
THANK YOU, GOD MY FATHER;
FOR ALL YOUR LOVE.

Chapter 4

My Star Flickers and Shines Bright – Boy or Girl or Both?

By Debere Worley
October 2004

I am now energetic, thoughtful and enthusiastic:

I am still trying to figure out Who Am I?

My thoughts derive from my childhood through my adulthood:

"It's a Boy"

- "I will, from this day forward, wear ethnic clothing and wear my hair in a short Afro style, along with my jewelry in gold."—I yam who I yam

Debere's very own glamour shot. Make up and hairstyle by her friend.

- "I will wear sandals in the summer and deer skin boots in the winter"
- "I will shine my star ever so brightly and follow in the footsteps of Jesus"

"I may have figured out the longtime self-mystery of who I am." I have been putting together all the mysterious serious cracks into one pile:

1. You are too good to be true . . .
2. You are my very special sister . . .
3. Some of these beauty salons only accept certain people
4. "Come on Debere—let's fight! I'm going to beat you! So come on." POP! SLAP! BOO! **The rambunctious person that has been hidden comes out! TIGER WORLEY!!!**
5. "I want to be just like you Mr. Heard, when I grow up. I like your style and your choices in life," said Willy Green.
6. "You are an angel from God," said Mark Webster, known as Minister Wench.
7. "You're rich," said by a gentlemen I first met in Reno, Nevada on a bus tour.

Now this is what they said when I was born: "IT IS A BOY. However, it has a missing part down below."

"We'll just turn it into a girl," said Mother Dorothy. "I already have one boy. So all I need is a girl and then I will have my American Dream! I will be the envy of the neighborhood. My boy and girl. My black cocker Spaniel, my future dream apartment and our handsome couple. No brag, just fact!"

However, I, Debere Worley, played the role as a girl and woman for 51 years. On October 21, 2004, I declared myself a young bachelor. I will be making arrangements to change my dress style and hair style. I do not choose to do any dating since I am not sexually compatible, due to missing parts. Oh well, I cannot have everything. I am still gorgeous . . .

I finally realize I am not gay. I am just identified as a girl, woman, black chick, etc.

I am just too good to be true. I really freak people out by the way I look and act. I look just like a beautiful woman. I walk and move like a woman. I talk like a woman. I am a woman. I just can't get pregnant. Why? Cause I am really a boy . . . I know it will be hard for you to see me any other way. However, you will have to in this life and not in the next.

Just look at it like this—My mother had no choice but to pretend that I was something that I was not. I even feel like a twin. I feel like a girl and I feel like a boy. I just want to be who I really am. That's me! I really never have felt right. Please help me keep my eyes on the prize.

So as of October 22, 2004, you can officially call me Debere (Debra) [JeanPierre Debre, Prime Minister of France 1948]. Oops, more slandered comments:

"You are not sorority material," said my brother Michael.

"You qualify more than I do for an inheritance," said my brother Michael. "Williamae has a problem with you Debere," said Frances.

"There is a reason why," said Gertrude.

"Your mother would be disappointed if she knew how you were living your life," said Orita

"We are really enjoying having you in our neighborhood," said Mrs. Wells. "I did not think that was a handicap," said Mrs. Wells.

And I could go on and on about all the comments being said to me in my life. I am looking back now to try to add up and understand the meaning of all these comments and ask myself:

"Now what do you get? Is it a Girl or a Boy."

Clearly I am confused and need help from God to understand the meaning of my life.

Chapter 5

I am so Truly Black and White

January 6, 2005

How did my mind manage to discover the truth?

I was holding the nice hard copy book in my hands, "1942-43 Who's Who in America"—a very nice and expensive book. BUT after holding it in the middle of my hand, the angel decided to let the book open up at page 423-424.

This was MY DESTINY given to me by God. For next, I started reading these pages that automatically opened to my eyes, and found a well known name of a famous person whom I often heard people speak about. This man had a very full and complete life. He manufactured something drastic and it changed his life. But then he turned into a recluse and lived a lonely life to the end. His name was **Howard Robard Hughes.**

He was one of the most successful men of his 1930s-1940s generation in the United States. He dated many movie stars and was one of America's most sought out bachelors. He was doing very well in life until he met a woman one day, who was a true fox. She was MY

So Bright My Shimmering Star

MOTHER. She was more gorgeous than any woman he ever met. Howard Hughes fell in love with her and had a little girl by her. She was born in 1953. Howard was very elated as his daughter took on all of his characteristics.

Debere was considered the golden child who grew up to be the prize of her family and a real princess at heart.

Her name was DEBERE—and she had his dark and penetrating eyes. Her nose, mouth and ears were just like Howard Hughes. He saw her often during the first two years. After that, no one heard from him again. He stopped having pictures taken and let his hair grow very long and his nails impossibly long—during his years of reclusive abandonment of the world. Yes, he became insane and paranoid.

Howard Hughes love of a Melado lady produced Debere—the Melado girl. This scared Howard into seclusion. He then feared how the world might think of him in that era. A mind is a terrible thing to waste. Anxiety then creeped in and then tore this great giant apart. The country was not ready to hear about a Caucasian billionaire, who was falling in love with a Melado woman and having a Melado child. Since Lincoln was responsible for ending slavery, that was not suppose to happen. Had the rich entrepreneur lost his cotton-picking mind? What price would he have to pay for going back to a Plantation setting? He could not handle this position he put himself into. He was going crazy and lost all hope and enthusiasm in his life. He had no remaining reason to live and enjoy life. His fear took over and destroyed him.

PLEASE UNDERSTAND: Howard Hughes had many disguises; Before he totally lost his mind, he would come and see his baby girl. His baby was the only one he would see, for she was truly his pride and joy.

A Gifted Man Produced a Gifted Child

Howard saw Debere graduate from Bowling Green State University. Afterwards, Howard died and made history as one of the greatest men that ever lived. We shall always remember him as the greatest and implant his greatness in all of our own children's lives. A movie is now being made of Howard Hughes and his experiences, for November 2005 release to the world.

Debere is now age 51 and will be featured in Ebony's magazine:
TO THE GREAT ONE
For he is a jolly good fellow
For he is a jolly good fellow
For he is a jolly good fellow

That nobody can deny
That nobody can deny
That nobody can deny

For he is a jolly good fellow . . .
That nobody can ever deny

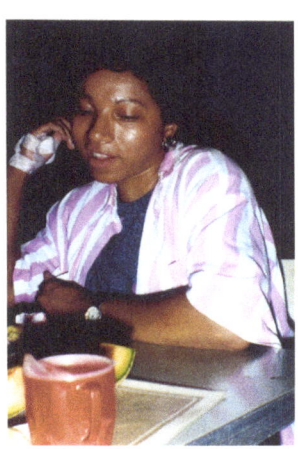

Ouch!!! That sure did hurt. I burned my right hand while cooking in the kitchen.

Another Clue

My left pinkie finger was broken while riding in Howard's powered limousine. My finger was still on the window when the driver was closing the window. I cried with extreme pain. However, I was not taken to a medical center or emergency room, since Howard made the decision that I was OK.

But my finger grew crooked thereafter. I have never had another limo ride opportunity during my adult life. Maybe that is why I am sad?

Please enjoy this chapter.

MY MIND AND MY SOUL WORKS IN WONDROUS WAYS.

Chapter 6

My Wonderful Mom

Debere Worley
April 2002

Always Still Watching Over Me

When I come Home, I feel your presence all around.

When I go upstairs to your bedroom, I sense your being on all,
Things that I touch and on all that I see.

When I gaze unto the mirror on the dresser wall,
I can see your radiant beauty prevailing over all.

When I sit in your rocking chair I always recall
How you held me close as a baby, when I was small.

When I stare at your night stand I smell your perfume,
And see your tissues throughout the room.

When I sit on your cedar chest, I see and feel

So Bright My Shimmering Star

Kathy, Debere, Mama Dorothy, and my mother's dear friend, John.

All the heirlooms which you so proudly kept,
And I see your Chester drawer where you kneeled
Down to me as a child, when I wept,

And I see the classic Singer sewing machine
Where you created so many pretty garments
In the wonderful image of yourself.

Now I miss your presence Mom, and I sometimes weep
All day, all night and in my sleep,
Because I miss you so much.

But I know you are still here with me still,
Because the joy and thrill you provide to me in your room,
Brings me back to happiness,
And your spirit brings life to my soul.

Thank you Mama for giving to me

My Wonderful Mom

So many precious memories
Which shall live with me the rest of my life.

You were my best friend,
And I shall cherish the essence of your love and caring,
The rest of my life here on earth
Before we meet again in heaven.

I will always love my Mama;
In the end, she was my baby girl,
As I was hers.

Chapter 7

Flight 911: Saving The World, Pass it Foward

By Debere Worley
September 24, 2002

I struggle every day to survive my chemistry and fears. I sometimes receive help from my Big Bear friend to perform my self-hypnosis, put my feet on the ground and to reach out to the world. It works for me, and I wish to "Pass it Forward."

Dear Big Bear,

Little Bear here. Just prowling by to drop a few lines on you.
Baby . . . I think the chemistry experiment you conducted may conclude to be very important for medical history. The successful conclusion of the experiment, may lead to the saving of many lives. I wish to Pass Forward that blessing to others.
I am now putting everything slowly together . . . My Godmother, Dr. Ella P. Stewart left a legacy in me. Her one and only daughter died. I don't know what she died of, but I perceive it may have something

in relation to a severe chemical unbalance. She, in turn, was asked to be the godmother of a baby girl that had an identical background as her daughter: chemically, racial—including Cherokee Indian, African American, . . . Yes, I am putting all the pieces together. Yes, I would love to be chosen as the people's princess—so I could help all the people who suffer from severe chemical imbalances.

I am very pleased with your contributions. You will be blessed by the almighty God for your deliverance.

My father once worked for a very wealthy Caucasian family that had a child that suffered from a severe chemical imbalance. He became vice-president of his father's company, successfully married a wealthy and prominent young diva, and had a son and daughter, who he became so proud of. However, he met disaster one morning that led to his death. His wife tried to protect him, by hiding his car keys—to keep him from driving his car, due to severe inebriation (which had taken place during a party his wife had for him in celebration of his birthday). He had no idea of knowing this would be the final and last time he would be celebrating his birthday with family and friends.

I actually believe that this family donated over a million dollars to research this deadly condition, which we now refer to as "bipolar." It is a condition which has affected one out of eight people in our society. I believe this family has contributed to the some of those professional therapist who have been helpful to my survival. It is very important in our society, here at large, that I also continue to survive—so I can teach others what I have learned:

- Maintain Positive Thinking – that is a personal choice we have the power to make for ourselves, if we believe.
- Never Give Up Living – live is precious; life is happiness and joy; life is what we wish it to be; we need only to reach out to others with love, to make it happen.

Flight 911: Saving The World, Pass it Foward

Chin was a classmate of mine; and majored in electrical engineering at UT.

These lessons may help people, of all types, but also with this chemical unbalance condition, to live longer than they ever have.

Now I am almost certain that it was not by accident, that a certain African-American lady, sat next to a certain Jewish-Caucasian man on a Northwest Airlines flight, one sun-shiny afternoon. His sincerity, integrity and tenacity in sustaining human life substance—was observed by myself, and we became friends—resulting in my survival today. This may result in a breakthrough for mankind . . . If I can successfully PASS IT FORWARD.

I thank you Big Bear for contributing to mankind. You are a true prince for civilization.

. . .This chapter of my book must be called "Flight 911." The man and the lady involved with this impact, will continue to live happily ever after, with their families and friends, and be two of the most protected individuals around.

So Bright My Shimmering Star

    I Believe in Life Everlasting Forever . . .
    "Little Bear"

    Lil Bear finds Big Bear—With Love From God—Lil Bear still has Big Bear friendship.

Chapter 8

Learning to Conquer Social Love and Fear: Inside and Outside at the Dinner Dance

Debere Worley's Journal
November 2, 2005

Traumatization Begins

My mind and soul certainly remember my traumatic experience at the dinner dance, Friday, October 28. WHY did this happen?

I must have been in a panic mood. Mild forces and events just messed with my mind that night. At first, I was devastated by not being able to find a seat in the dance hall. Marge was holding seats for her sons. Mrs. Bufkin told me that I could sit with her family. But looking for the family, I could not find them.

Then I recognized another lady, from the parking lot, going to the back of the hall. (I had parked near her and I had asked why everyone was leaving—so she said there was a time error in the flyer, so we all missed the mass event, being too late. Now we all were going directly to the Stranaham.) So I walked towards the back of the hall and saw this lady seated with a Philippine group. Now I was lucky and was able to sit back there the entire time.

Sick Cookie Prevails

But I still feel excessively disturbed—for missing the mass (which I wanted so much to attend), and thereby feeling in a bad condition of depression and fear. I also retained frustration for missing a good seat. So as a Sick Cookie, I had no courage to get up and leave; I was uncomfortable, miserable and unaware of the family I was sitting with.

Social Heavenly Mini-Event

Finally, Father Nelson appeared in front of me, recognized me and sat down with me. We had a pleasant conversation and he also spoke with others in the back. So then I was feeling relieved to socialize with God and the human race. But it did not last . . . He had to leave and I returned to my miserable sick Cookie feelings . . . until . . .

Beautiful Dancers Then Prevail

God my Father, continues to help me, as I watch everyone dancing and having fun. I begin to enjoy all the happiness and good times I am watching in all dancers and socializers. I see a beautiful lady dancing with her children, as her husband watched them from the table. My Joy increases as I realize how much I appreciated the beauty of the woman who loves to dance with her children. Why so beautiful???

Beautiful Baloons Strike My Mind

A more beautiful woman emerges from no-where, with beautiful balloons to give to children. The most beautiful woman I had ever

seen. Amazingly, she begins to remind me of myself:
- My love of balloons and of children
- My feeling at the moment as being a man, because
- My attraction to this woman must mean I am a man?

So I go the restroom.

Petrification Returns

When I return, all are gone. I immediately become fearful and petrified. So I quickly leave, with the string of a balloon attached to my foot. I had to stop and untangle the balloons. But I could not untangle my emotions.

I HAVE A RAPID MOOD DISORDER CHALLENGE. I AM FEELING THE HIGHS AND FEELING THE LOWS.

I quietly and politely walk away from the hall to my car, drive home to 941 Carver Blvd. Then I fed my kitty-cat a midnight snack, and I went to check on Mr. Heard. I stayed there at his house all night:
- thinking of the highs—the beautiful girl with the beautiful balloon. I am really attracted to her.
- feeling the lows—I could not sleep all night; I did not understand what was happening to me

Balancing My Mind

Now I have more time in the following days, to figure it out. I conclude that I have both a boy personality and a girl personality inside me. The boy powered the girl in me that night, at the Dinner Dance event.

Now I understand why I must take medicine—to keep my boy and girl personality and mood in balance, so I can correctly behave as the girl I really am supposed to be.

THANK YOU, GOD, MY FATHER, FOR HELPING ME.

PLEASE HELP ME UNDERSTAND FURTHER WHO AM I?

My dream is to always remain to be the girl that I am. Girls are supposed to be prettier than boys.

I had asked another girlfriend about the beautiful girl I admired at the party, and she told me that the girl was really a "he-she." I have eternally wondered whether I myself am also a 'he-she." The thought can make me lose my balance, lose my self-respect, lose my happiness . . .

Because I need to respect my self, I need to be a puritan, I need to be a good participant in human society. Some friends have told me I am a puritan to be proud of myself. But I still question myself forever . . . since I have no proof of mother or wife in this world.

PLEASE GOD, MY FATHER, HELP ME UNDERSTAND WHO I REALLY AM. SHOULD I BELIEVE MY FRIEND OR MY FEAR? PLEASE WHISPER THE TRUTH IN MY EAR . . . Thank you, Father.

Chapter 9

Poetic Memoirs of a Geisha

I Am Not as Great as You

    I am not as great as you
However I am human too
I congratulate you for all the work you do
However I do a different work that you could never do
So now I am as great as you
But your are as great as me
    Now is the time for us to live happily ever after
    However you are already living happily ever after!

Always in my Heart

    I am learning so many things now about life—even though I am not in college.
    I have learned that there is nothing

I am also blessed with the talents of a poetic princess. I love to recite poetry.

more precious than giving someone a piece of your heart.

I have learned that you have to put your thought into action, if you wish not to stand still

I have learned how to be happy and why it is so important to be.

I have learned how to open my eyes and see clearly now.

These are a few of my learnings which I plan to put into practice.

Even though I do not know where this wisdom is leading me to.

Even though I do not know how I am able to retain so much information in so little time.

But I do think I am involved in a master plan of my creator.

I cross my heart to God that I use my new learnings with wisdom and with God's grace.

My Plan Includes My Friend

I do believe that my master plan includes my dearest friend.

Who has no reason to fear the Creator.

The Creator is a friend of my dearest friend and a friend of the entire World created.

All I can do is to pray and meditate over everything that is happening now with my dearest friend and me. We are truly Children of The Universe.

God Our Father put us here to love everything he has created.

God Our Father created both of us.

I will always love God Our Father and love his created Son, my best friend, who will always love me, as taught to us by God.

I Will Hold Onto You Forever

Written by Debere Worley for Jenny Veres—June 14, 2000

You have left me with sorrow and grief; however, I will hold onto you forever.

You have left me alone with your two brothers and your dad.

We will miss you dearly and keep your memories alive.

I will always remember the happiness and joy you showed me when I presented you with a new pair of gym shoes.

You were my all and everything. How can I give you up? You were my special gift from God.

But I know that it gives me great joy to see you again when God shall call on me.

I will continue to live a good life, so that I can have the opportunity to see you for eternity.

You are my special baby who I shall always love forevermore.

Be good and do not forget, mama will always be there for you and will joyfully meet you one day at the Pearly Gates.

And Then Came Barry

And then came Barry with the truth and realism in life.

He was more than a stranger that sat down next to me on a Boeing 727 jet enroute to Los Angeles, California.

He was like an angel I met while flying in the sky. But I was not going to heaven. I was going to LA.

He became my best friend in reality. He was a loving and caring husband, father, grandfather, brother and uncle, residing in California.

Just think—if I had not missed my flight, I would not have met him. I am very proud to have met someone as great as Barry.

Yes I Fell In Love With You

Yes I fell in love with you.

I did not mean to—but I did.

Please do not punish me.

I was just being honest with my feelings for you.

I love everything about you from what I observe.
I wish you shall not burst my bubble by destroying my dream.
That is all I have to hold onto that is real to me.
So let me keep dreaming on for a while longer—
At least until I may wake up and call it a dream away from reality.

My Basket of Joy

My basket of joy today includes my father and my family. The basket grew with joy when my mother and father created my sisters, Barbara and Brenda and my brother, Bruce—"the 4 B's."

We all lived happily together in all kinds of weather. We studied and played and took up for one another together. We did everything as one family, within our basket of joy.

My dad spent lots of time teaching me my work ethics of life, by taking me to work at 1:30 a.m. on weekends and in the summers. He introduced me to many different types of people—to know and to understand and to love. He helped me learn how to work, to stand strong, to help others, to create achievements by action, which speaks louder than words.

He also taught me how to forgive and forget.

My basket of joy continued to grow as I became a man and created a family of my own in California—two daugthers, one son, and four grandchildren. Now we are all adults.

I am proud to repeat the strengths that my dad taught me. And now I shall teach strength and love to my grandchildren.

Thank you, God our Father, for allowing me to love and appreciate and follow the jewels of behavior, which my dad gave me in my basket of joy.

I WILL ALWAYS LOVE MY DAD AND GOD OUR FATHER FROM THE BOTTOM OF MY HEART AS MY BASKET OF JOY.

Chapter 10

Life is a Rainbow

April 12, 2002

Life is a Rainbow—if you look through the rainclouds
And pursue the distant magnificent shapes and colors:
Life can be a joyful merry-go-round
If you decide to ignore the spin and love the twirl
Life is a giant pond for uplifting bliss
If you have the will to always kiss your life,
And worship the family and friends about you
Life can really be what you wish it to be—
As you ignore the trash and instead reach for and see the sky,
As you gaze above the rough ground to see your mind's eye,
As you focus on your love of life and create
Just a small piece of your dreams—as God does for you-
Which is all you really need to be Happy.
For Life is the Rainbow, as you choose to see,
Life is the Rainbow, as you choose to love,
Life is the person, whomever you choose to Be.

So Bright My Shimmering Star

Happy Earth Day and Happy Birthday to Debere

Debere and classmate Lee from Taiwan. We both were working on a masters degree at the University of Toledo.

Debere is living the dream while gazing at the water near Putin bay.

Life is a Rainbow

Debere and Lee making the perfect pose. We made a promise that we would meet up to see each other again in the near future.

My classmates Jeanet and Joseph graduate from the Unversity of Toledo in early May.

Debere, Satita and Kathy living the educational dream that is king.

So Bright My Shimmering Star

Debere and best friend Kathy standing at the docks in Putin Bay.

Debere and neighbor Jevona on Earth Day which is also Debere's birthday, April 22.

Debere and classmate Satita giving the peace sign. We both majored in Educational Technology with emphasis in computers. I would like to visit her in China someday.

Life is a Rainbow

Debere with team leader at the Edison plant in Toledo, OH

Debere with class of teachers visting the Davis Bessie Nuclear plant. We are looking forward to bringing new ideas to the classroom.

Debere, her professor and classmates at the University of Toledo. Ed585–Great Process in Education

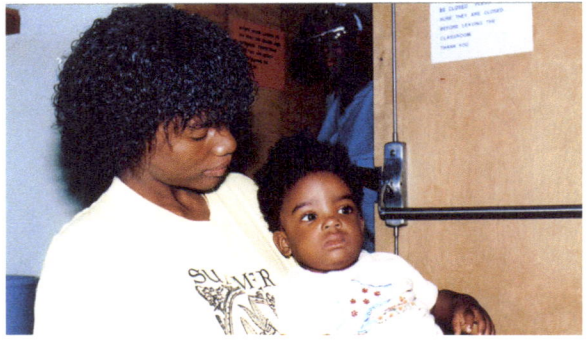

Joseph's wife, Katie holds her daughter while waiting for her husband.

Chapter 11

New Vision: Now My Life Torch Is Ever So Brightly Shining

We all remember these words from an American president, John Kennedy, the 35th president of the United States of America: "Ask not what your country can do for you. Ask what you can do for your country!"

President Kennedy deeply loved our country—as much as he loved my Godmother, whom I have now discovered may really be my Grandmother.

My Grandmother was equivalently married to him for three years.

During this time she traveled around the world as an American

Debere at her parents' gravesite in Woodlawn Cemetary, Toledo, OH.

43

Ambassador. This was the part of history that was unknown, to all the world. It was certainly unknown to me also.

But now God My Father, has recently allowed me to create the Vision of My Emerging Existence.

My Vision began after been given a crystal oil lantern, designed with the wings of an eagle—in flight to infinity. The name "EAGLE" was inscribed in the brass ring at the base of the crystal lantern.

This will make the crystal set complete, along with my Godmother's lantern in the matching crystal pattern. Now . . . Let us look at the Life That Took Place Many Years Ago . . .

The Torch Is Passed and must be placed where it truly belongs.

I will try, with all my heart, and very soon, to bring The EAGLE Torch To Its Proper Home—that must relate to my Grandmother and her Love of the World.

Dear Lord, please teach me how to present the EAGLE Torch.

Dear precious Lord, with all my heart, please lead me on—to the future. Please take my hand. I am weak, I am weary. I am worn. Please take my hand to help carry the torch to help the world, that loves thee Lord.

My grandfather has lovingly led us to where we are now. We have come a long way. He would be so proud of us now.

The country of the United States has the big EAGLE at its side.

We are the greatest country that has ever existed in this whole world.

I myself, love this country. It is the greatest country ever, of all.

I am Debere, granddaughter created by my grandfather. I thank God for giving our country his grace to live here on the greatest land He has created.

Now I wish to pass the EAGLE Torch to the next Generation of youth, who are prepared to lead our country towards peace, freedom

New Vision: Now My Life Torch Is Ever So Brightly Shining

and liberty for all races all over the world.

This must be what we all must believe in and Create. The Torches for:

FREEDOM
EQUALITY
LOVE
BELIEF IN GOD, OUR REAL ORIGINAL BEST FATHER

THANK YOU, GOD MY FATHER

True Friends are like Diamonds,
So Precious and Rare.

False Friends are like Autumn Leaves,
That Fall from the Trees.

True Friends are like Diamonds,
So Precious and Rare.

False Friends are like Autumn Leaves,
That Fall from the Trees.

True Friends are like Diamonds,
So Precious and Rare.

False Friends are like Autumn Leaves,
That Fall from the Trees.

So Bright My Shimmering Star

Debere and Raymond realized that they were soulmates

Debere and Raymond sitting in the dining room at 941 Carver Boulevard, Toledo Ohio

In Loving Memory of
Raymond Heard
January 9, 1927 — March 9, 2011

www.ingramcontent.com/pod-product-compliance
Lightning Source LLC
Chambersburg PA
CBHW042338150426
43195CB00001B/38